My Very Own

HALLOWEEN

A Book of
Cooking and Crafts

My Very Own

HOLIDAY

BOOKS

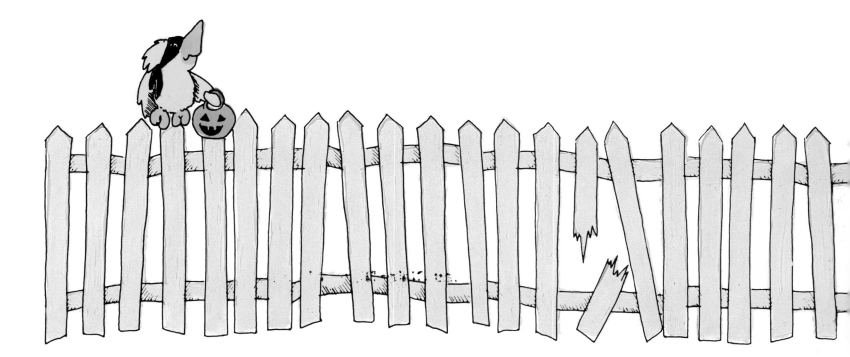

My Very Own

HALLOWEEN

A Book of Cooking and Crafts

by Robin West

photographs by Robert L. and Diane Wolfe
illustrations by Susan Slattery Burke

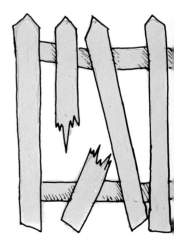

Carolrhoda Books, Inc./Minneapolis

To Mary Jo and Walter

Carolrhoda Books, Inc. c/o The Lerner Group
241 First Avenue North, Minneapolis, MN 55401

Library of Congress Cataloging-in-Publication Data

West, Robin.
   My very own Halloween : a book of cooking and
crafts / Robin West.
      p.   cm. — (My very own holiday books)
   Includes index.
   Summary: Contains recipes and crafts grouped
conveniently for five Halloween theme parties.
   ISBN 0-87614-725-2
   1. Cookery—Juvenile literature. 2. Handicraft—
Juvenile literature. 3. Halloween decorations—Juvenile
literature. 4. Entertaining—Juvenile literature.
[1. Halloween. 2. Cookery. 3. Parties.] I. Title. II. Series.
TX652.5.W45   1993
793.2'1—dc20   92—4543
                                                   CIP
                                                   AC

Manufactured in the United States of America

2 3 4 5 6 7 8 9 10 – I/HP – 01 00 99 98 97 96 95 94

Contents

Halloween Greetings / 7

Make It Your Very Own: How to Use this Book / 8

Cooking Smart / 10

Witch's Brew / 13

Spaced Out / 25

Creepy Crawlies / 33

Monster Meal / 41

Orange and Black Feast / 53

Recipe List / 62

Glossary / 63

Index / 64

My Very Own HALLOWEEN

Halloween Greetings

The night is dark and quiet, except for the howl of the wind blowing through the trees. There is a flash of white—a ghost! Or is it just a sheet hanging on a line? A bird cackles in a tree—or is it a witch? You never know, for this is a night for black cats and grinning pumpkins, creeping goblins and haunted houses. This is Halloween!

You don't have to wait until October 31 for the Halloween fun to begin. Getting ready for Halloween can be almost as much fun as the holiday itself. Make a spooky centerpiece for the table or a creepy character to sit in your window. You might even try having a party and making the food yourself (with a little help from an adult friend). The ideas are endless, so you'd better get started, because Halloween will be here before you know it!

Make It Your Very Own:
How to Use this Book

RECIPES

The recipes in this book are divided into five menus, but you don't have to make a whole meal.
If you are a new cook, start slowly. Choose a recipe that sounds good to you and try it out. You might need lots of help to begin with, but be patient. The more you practice, the better you'll be.

Here are some of the easier recipes to get you started:

Transylvania Tuna
Green Eye Pie
Cheese Fingers
Rocket Orange Punch

Once you know what you're doing, it's time to make a whole meal. Try one of the menus or put together your own combination.

Here are some things to consider when planning a menu:

Nutrition: Balance your menu by choosing something from each of the four food groups: breads, dairy products, fruits and vegetables, and meat and other proteins. You can fill out your menu with foods that don't need recipes, such as bread, fresh fruit, milk, cheese, and raw vegetables.

Variety: Include different tastes and textures in your meal. If one food is soft and creamy, serve it with something crunchy. Salty foods taste good when served with something sweet. Try to include a variety of colors so the food is as pretty to look at as it is good to eat.

Theme: Each of the menus in this

book has a theme, just to make it more fun. Try to think up a theme of your own, and choose recipes that go with it. How about a menu of foods that can be eaten with your fingers? (Of course, the first recipe on your list would have to be Cheese Fingers.) Why not serve a meal made up of green foods? Or forget about planning a meal, and make a variety of desserts instead. Anything is possible!

Be sure to share your masterpiece with someone else. Whether you make one dish or an entire meal, half the fun of cooking is watching someone else enjoy the food.

CRAFTS

Like the recipes, all of the crafts in this book are easy to make, but some are easier than others. If you haven't tried making crafts before, start with something easy, like a Spooky Spider or a Haunted Alien.

As you gain confidence, put together Gertrude the Geometric Witch or a Jack-o'-Lantern Candle. Once you've tackled these crafts, you're ready for Freaky Frankenstein.

Don't be afraid to use your imagination when decorating your crafts. Use markers, colored construction paper, scraps of fabric, or even glitter to give your craft a personal touch.

Cooking Smart

There's nothing like a good scare on Halloween, but you don't want it to happen when you're cooking. Whether you are a new or experienced cook, these cooking tips can help you avoid a kitchen disaster.

BEFORE YOU COOK

- Get yourself ready. If you have long hair, tie it back to keep it out of the food, away from flames, and out of your way. Roll up your sleeves, and put on an apron. And be sure to wash your hands well with soap.
- Read through the entire recipe and assemble all of the ingredients. It's no fun to find out halfway through a recipe that you're out of eggs.
- Go through the recipe with an adult helper and decide which steps you can perform yourself and which you'll need help with.

WHILE YOU COOK

- Raw meat and raw eggs can contain dangerous bacteria. Wash your hands and any utensils or cutting boards you've used after handling these raw foods. Never put cooked meat on an unwashed plate that has held raw meat. Any dough that contains raw eggs isn't safe to eat until it's cooked.
- Keep cold foods in the refrigerator until you need them.
- Wash fruits and vegetables thoroughly before using them.
- Turn pot handles to the back of the stove so the pots won't be knocked off by accident. When you are taking the lid off a hot pan, always keep the opening away from your face so the steam won't burn you.
- Use a potholder when handling hot pans. Be sure the potholder is

dry before you use it. The heat from the pan will come right through a wet potholder.

• Always turn off the stove or oven as soon as you're done with it.
• Be careful with foods when they come out of the microwave. Although the food may seem to be cool to the touch, microwaving can produce hot spots. When you're heating a liquid in the microwave, stir it often to distribute the heat evenly.
• Use only microwave-safe dishes in the microwave. Never put anything metal in the microwave.
• Don't cut up food in your hand, use a cutting board.
• Carry knives point down.
• Be careful when opening cans, the edges of the lids are very sharp.
• Don't save the mess for the end, try to clean up as you go along.

AFTER YOU COOK

• Once you've finished cooking, be sure to store your creation in the refrigerator if it contains any ingredients that might spoil.
• Be a courteous cook: clean up your mess. Leave the kitchen looking as clean as (or cleaner than) you found it.

SOME CRAFTY TIPS

Assembling a craft is a lot like cooking, and many of the same tips apply. Read the instructions and gather your supplies before you start. Play it safe with your supplies, especially scissors, and be sure to get an adult friend to help you when you need it. Put down newspapers to protect your work surface. And, of course, be sure to clean up your mess when you're done.

Witch's Brew

Bubbling Cauldron Chili

▼

Cheese Fingers

▼

Witch's Hair Slaw

▼

Magic Center Cupcakes

▼

*Gertrude the
Geometric Witch*

au Claire District L

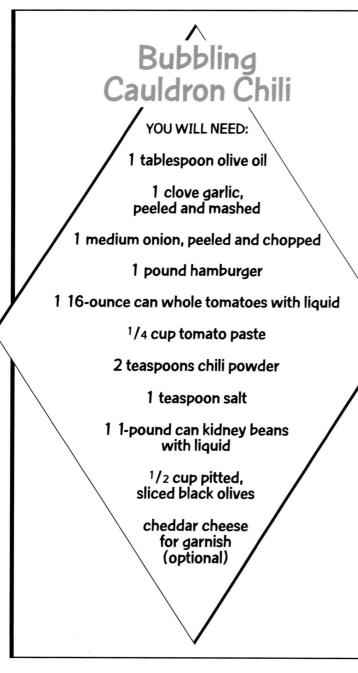

Bubbling Cauldron Chili

YOU WILL NEED:

1 tablespoon olive oil

1 clove garlic,
peeled and mashed

1 medium onion, peeled and chopped

1 pound hamburger

1 16-ounce can whole tomatoes with liquid

1/4 cup tomato paste

2 teaspoons chili powder

1 teaspoon salt

1 1-pound can kidney beans
with liquid

1/2 cup pitted,
sliced black olives

cheddar cheese
for garnish
(optional)

1. In a large kettle, combine olive oil, garlic, and onion. Cook over medium heat, stirring often, until onion is transparent.

2. Add the hamburger and break it up into small pieces. Cook, stirring often, until meat is brown. Drain off the grease.

3. Add tomatoes, tomato paste, chili powder, and salt, and stir well.

4. Cook, uncovered, over medium-low heat for 30 minutes, stirring occasionally.

5. Add beans and olives, and continue cooking for 20 minutes or until bubbly.

6. Sprinkle dishes of chili with cheese before serving.

Serves 4

Bubbling Cauldron Chili is also terrific served with Cheese Fingers instead of cheddar cheese.

Cheese Fingers

YOU WILL NEED:

3 slices white bread

3/4 cup grated cheddar cheese

3 tablespoons grated Parmesan cheese

3 tablespoons milk

1 Preheat oven to 400°.

2 Remove crusts from bread. Discard crusts.

3 With your hands, break bread into small pieces and drop into medium bowl.

4 Add cheeses and milk to bread. Mix well with hands, kneading the bread into the cheese, until dough will hold the shape of a ball.

5 Roll heaping teaspoons of mixture into 15 fingers and arrange on an ungreased cookie sheet.

6 Bake for 10 to 12 minutes or until fingers begin to turn brown.

Makes 15 Cheese Fingers

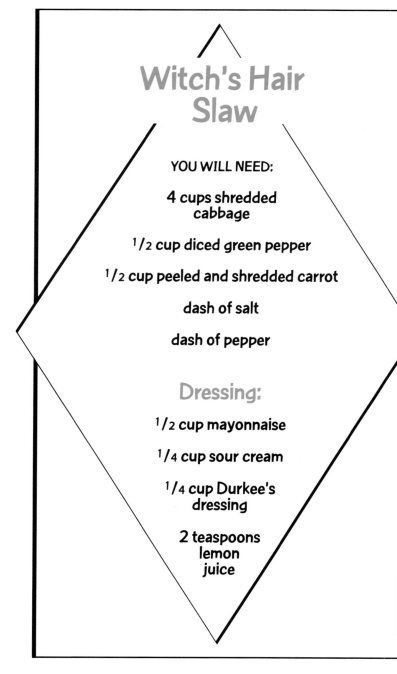

Witch's Hair Slaw

YOU WILL NEED:

4 cups shredded cabbage

$1/2$ cup diced green pepper

$1/2$ cup peeled and shredded carrot

dash of salt

dash of pepper

Dressing:

$1/2$ cup mayonnaise

$1/4$ cup sour cream

$1/4$ cup Durkee's dressing

2 teaspoons lemon juice

1. In a large bowl, combine cabbage, green pepper, and carrot and mix well.

2. In a small bowl, combine mayonnaise, sour cream, Durkee's dressing, and lemon juice. Stir well.

3. Pour the dressing over the cabbage mixture and mix well.

4. Stir in salt and pepper.

5. Refrigerate for at least an hour before serving.

Serves 4 to 6

You can substitute ½ to ¾ cup bottled coleslaw dressing for the dressing in this recipe.

Does Your Cat Sneeze When It Rains?

You may have heard that Friday the 13th is unlucky and so is walking under a ladder or breaking a mirror. Or someone might have told you that carrying a rabbit's foot or finding a four-leafed clover will bring you good luck. These are all superstitions. While most people don't really believe in superstitions, you might catch them being a little more careful every time Friday the 13th comes around.

Here are some less common superstitions:

- If your cat sneezes, it will rain.
- If a woman cuts a slice of homemade bread and the slice doesn't fall apart, she will marry the man she loves.
- If your big toe itches, company is coming.
- If you sleep on the same pillow as your dog, you will have the same dreams.
- Sleeping on a table is bad luck.
- If you carry a newborn baby upstairs before you carry the baby downstairs, the child will be a success.
- If your palm itches, you will receive money soon. If the bottom of your foot itches, you will be going on a trip.

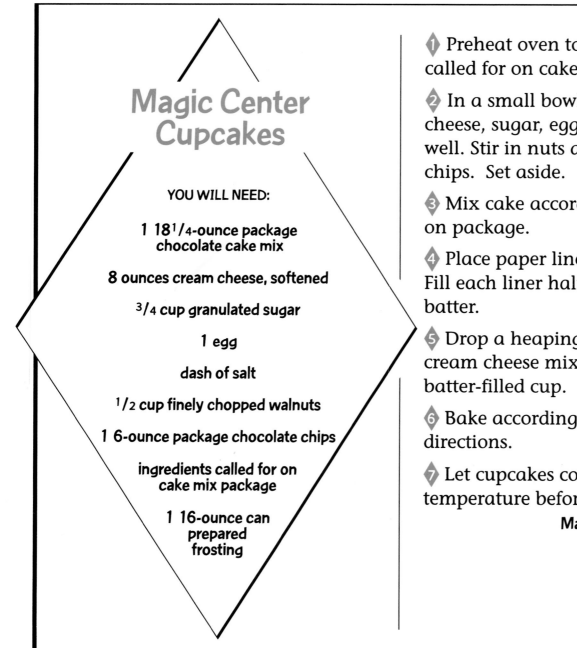

Magic Center Cupcakes

YOU WILL NEED:

1 18^1/$_4$-ounce package chocolate cake mix

8 ounces cream cheese, softened

^{3}/$_4$ cup granulated sugar

1 egg

dash of salt

^{1}/$_2$ cup finely chopped walnuts

1 6-ounce package chocolate chips

ingredients called for on cake mix package

1 16-ounce can prepared frosting

1. Preheat oven to temperature called for on cake mix package.

2. In a small bowl, combine cream cheese, sugar, egg, and salt and stir well. Stir in nuts and chocolate chips. Set aside.

3. Mix cake according to directions on package.

4. Place paper liners in muffin pan. Fill each liner half full of cake batter.

5. Drop a heaping teaspoon of the cream cheese mixture into each batter-filled cup.

6. Bake according to package directions.

7. Let cupcakes cool to room temperature before frosting.

Makes 30 to 36 cupcakes

Gertrude the Geometric Witch

YOU WILL NEED:

tracing paper

pencil

construction paper

scissors

ruler

white liquid glue

masking tape

cardboard scrap at least
3 inches by 3 inches

yarn

12-inch pipe cleaner

THE BODY:

1 Place tracing paper on top of figure A on page 20 and trace. Cut out tracing paper pattern. Place pattern on construction paper and trace around it. Cut out construction paper body.

2 Mark construction paper body with dots pictured on figure A. With a ruler, draw lines to connect dots as shown. Fold on these lines, keeping the lines on the inside of the folds.

3 Glue tab 1 to flap X, tab 2 to flap Y, and tab 3 to flap X. The tabs should be glued to the inside. You have formed a three-dimensional triangle.

THE LEGS:

1 Use a ruler to draw four 18- by 1-inch rectangles on construction paper. Cut out rectangles.

2 Glue strip 1 to strip 2 to form an

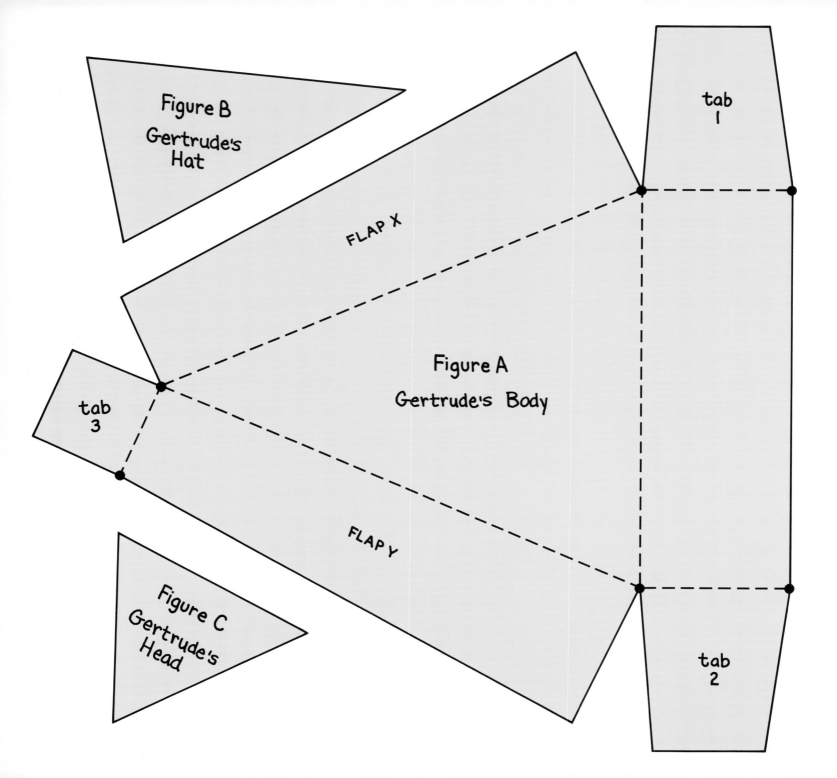

Figure B
Gertrude's
Hat

tab
1

FLAP X

Figure A

Gertrude's Body

tab
3

FLAP Y

Figure C
Gertrude's
Head

tab
2

L shape. Leave 1 inch at the end of the strip 1 as shown. This extra inch of paper is the leg tab.

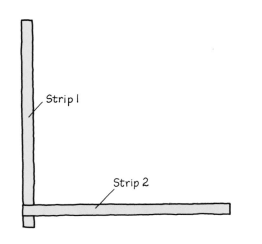

3 Fold strip 1 over strip 2 and crease. Then fold strip 2 over strip 1 and crease.

4 Repeat step 3 until you run out of paper.

5 Glue the ends of the two strips together.

6 Repeat steps 2 through 5 to make the second leg.

THE ARMS:

1 Use a ruler to draw four 12- by 1-inch rectangles on construction paper. Cut out rectangles.

2 Glue two strips together to form an L shape as shown. (Don't leave an inch at the bottom as you did with the legs.)

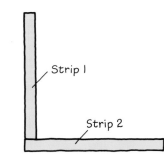

3 Fold and glue the strips according to steps 3 through 5 of the leg instructions.

4 Repeat to make second arm.

THE HEAD AND HAT:

1 Place tracing paper on top of figures B and C on page 20 and trace. Cut out tracing paper patterns. Place patterns on construction paper and trace around them. Cut out construction paper head and hat.

2 Use a ruler to draw a 3¼- by ½-inch rectangle on construction paper. This is the brim of the hat. Cut out rectangle.

3 Glue the head and hat to the brim as shown.

TO ASSEMBLE:

1 Glue the head and hat to the top of the body.

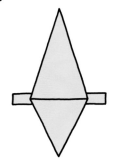

2 Glue the arms to the side of the triangle about halfway down. Hold each arm in place until the glue sets.

3 Glue leg tabs to the underside of the body. Tape them to make them extra secure.

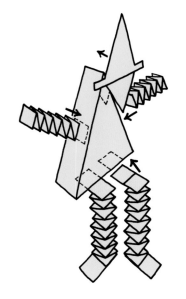

THE BROOM:

1 Use a ruler to draw a 3- by 3-inch square on the cardboard. Cut out square.

2 Wrap yarn around the square 15 times.

3 Cut through the yarn along one edge of the square and remove square. You will have 15 6-inch pieces of yarn.

4 Bend the pipe cleaner in half.

5 Gather the yarn in the middle and wrap the bent pipe cleaner around it. Twist pipe cleaner until you come to the end.

6 Tie the base of the broom with a short piece of yarn to secure.

TO DECORATE:

Use circles, rectangles, and triangles to give Gertrude eyes, nose, and a mouth. You can make hands out of construction paper and glue them to the ends of her arms. Don't forget those wicked red fingernails, made with small rectangles. Use yarn to make her scraggly hair.

Spaced Out

Unidentified Flying Pancake
▼
Lunar Cheese and Apple Casserole
▼
Rocket Orange Punch
▼
Frozen Space Orbs
▼
Haunted Aliens

USS PUMPKIN

Unidentified Flying Pancake

YOU WILL NEED:

$1/2$ cup milk

2 eggs

$1/2$ cup flour

1 tablespoon butter or margarine

1 cup sliced strawberries or chopped ham or applesauce for filling

maple syrup

powdered sugar (optional)

1. Preheat oven to 425°.

2. In a medium bowl, beat together milk and eggs. Add flour and stir until smooth.

3. Place butter in a 9-inch pie pan and heat in oven for 1 to 2 minutes or until butter is melted.

4. Remove pie pan from oven and pour batter into pan.

5. Bake for 12 minutes or until pancake is firm in the middle and golden brown on the edges.

6. Flip pancake onto a serving dish. Spread filling evenly over pancake and roll up. Roll pancake as soon as it is cool enough to touch. If you wait too long, it will crack.

7. Serve with syrup. If you have used a sweet filling, dust with powdered sugar.

Serves 2

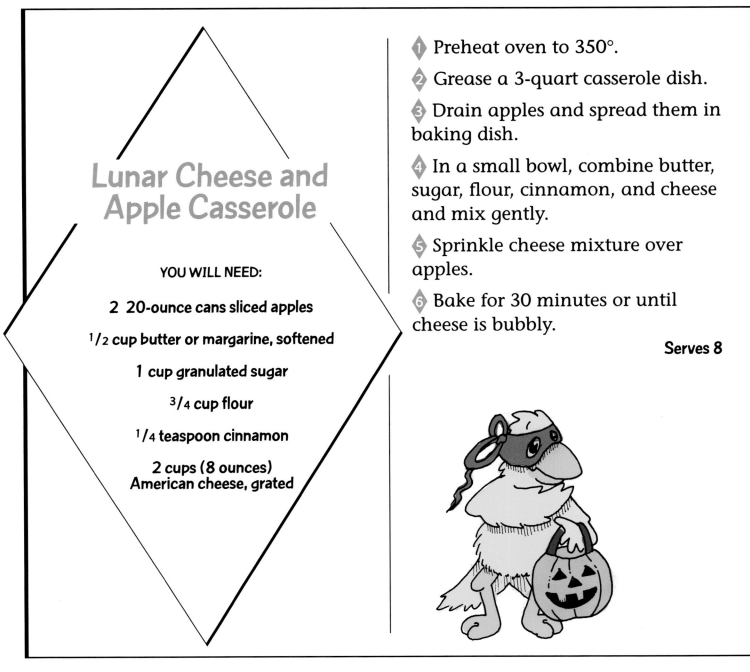

Lunar Cheese and Apple Casserole

YOU WILL NEED:

2 20-ounce cans sliced apples

$^1/_2$ cup butter or margarine, softened

1 cup granulated sugar

$^3/_4$ cup flour

$^1/_4$ teaspoon cinnamon

2 cups (8 ounces)
American cheese, grated

1. Preheat oven to 350°.

2. Grease a 3-quart casserole dish.

3. Drain apples and spread them in baking dish.

4. In a small bowl, combine butter, sugar, flour, cinnamon, and cheese and mix gently.

5. Sprinkle cheese mixture over apples.

6. Bake for 30 minutes or until cheese is bubbly.

Serves 8

Rocket Orange Punch

YOU WILL NEED:

1 6-ounce can unsweetened
frozen orange juice concentrate

1 cup milk

1 cup water

$1/4$ to $1/2$ cup granulated sugar

$1/2$ teaspoon vanilla

10 to 12 ice cubes

1 Combine all ingredients in a blender.

2 Blend 45 to 60 seconds or until ice cubes are crushed.

Serves 2 to 4

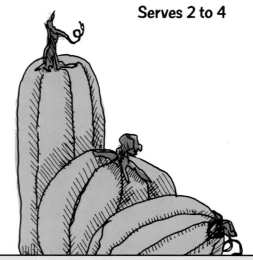

Reverse Trick or Treat:
A Halloween Game

Give each of the players a bag with 10 pieces of wrapped candy in it. Have the players write their names on their bags so the bags don't get mixed up. Decide on a time limit. If you are giving a party, you could keep the game going the

Frozen Space Orbs

YOU WILL NEED:

1 pint ice cream

16 to 20 chocolate wafer cookies

1 Place ice cream in a large bowl and stir to soften.

2 Spread about ¼ cup ice cream onto chocolate cookie and top with another cookie. Repeat with remaining ice cream and cookies.

3 Wrap cookies with foil and freeze 24 hours.

Makes 8 to 10 cookies

entire time, even while you are doing other things.

The object of the game is to catch people saying one of the following words:

Halloween   **candy**

witch   **party**

ghost   **pumpkin**

(It might be helpful to write the words in large letters on a piece of paper and tape the paper up where everyone can see it.) If you catch someone saying one of the words on the list, that person has to give you a piece of candy. The person who has the most candy at the end of the game wins a prize. And, of course, everyone gets to keep any candy he or she has left. Good luck!

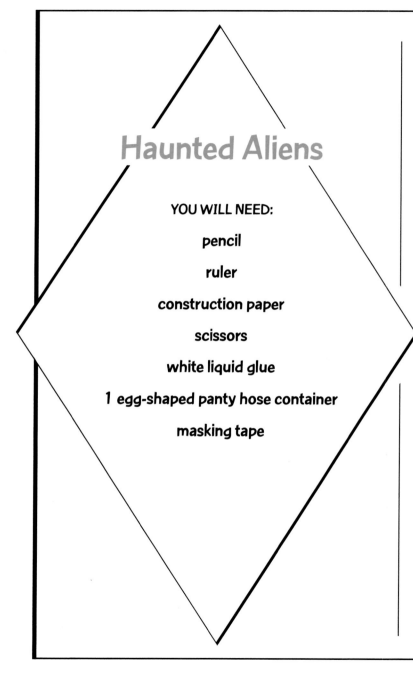

Haunted Aliens

YOU WILL NEED:

pencil

ruler

construction paper

scissors

white liquid glue

1 egg-shaped panty hose container

masking tape

1 Draw a 1- by 9-inch strip on the construction paper and cut it out.

2 Form this strip into a circle and glue the ends together, letting the ends overlap about 2 inches. This is the base.

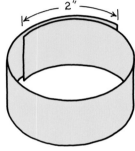

3 Cut shapes out of construction paper and glue them onto the plastic egg to give your haunted alien a face.

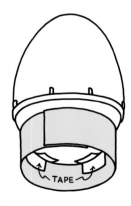

4 To attach your alien to its base, cut three pieces of masking tape and attach them to the inside of the base as shown.

5 Place the base against the more rounded end of the egg and press the masking tape down onto the egg.

USS PUMPKIN

Creepy Crawlies

Caterpillar Sandwich
▼
Peachy Spider Salad
▼
Dead but Delicious Grasshoppers
▼
Gooey Apple Treat
▼
Spooky Spiders

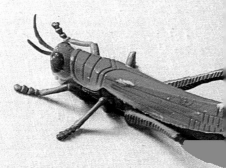

Caterpillar Sandwich

YOU WILL NEED:

1/4 cup mayonnaise

2 teaspoons parsley

2 teaspoons prepared mustard

1/4 teaspoon onion powder

1 loaf Italian bread

10 to 12 slices luncheon meat

10 to 12 slices cheese

1 Preheat oven to 375°.

2 In a small bowl, combine mayonnaise, parsley, mustard, and onion powder. Stir well and set aside.

3 Cut the bread into 10 slices without cutting all the way through the loaf.

4 Spread mayonnaise mixture between every other slice.

5 Fold the luncheon meat in half and tuck a slice of cheese in between. Insert folded meat and cheese into every slot that has the mayonnaise mixture in it.

6 Wrap the loaf in foil and bake for 25 minutes.

7 To serve, cut the loaf in slices at the cuts you didn't fill.

Makes 5 large sandwiches

Peachy Spider Salad

YOU WILL NEED:

1 canned peach half

1 carrot, peeled

2 raisins

1 cherry, sliced into a strip

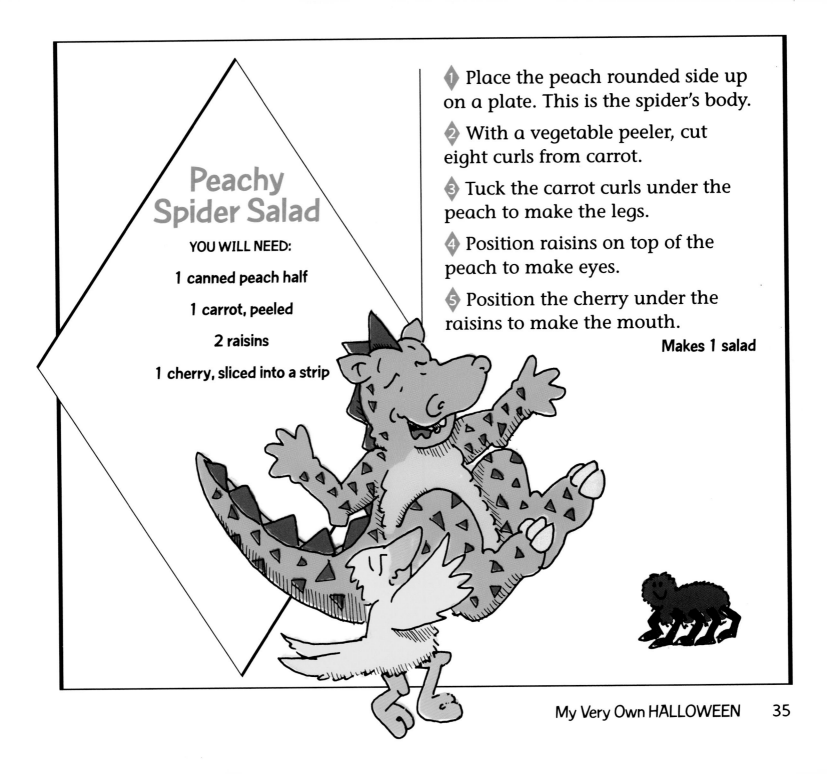

1. Place the peach rounded side up on a plate. This is the spider's body.

2. With a vegetable peeler, cut eight curls from carrot.

3. Tuck the carrot curls under the peach to make the legs.

4. Position raisins on top of the peach to make eyes.

5. Position the cherry under the raisins to make the mouth.

Makes 1 salad

Dead but Delicious Grasshoppers

YOU WILL NEED:

1 6-ounce package butterscotch chips

1 cup salted peanuts

3 cups chow mein noodles

1 In a medium saucepan, melt butterscotch pieces over low heat, stirring constantly. To microwave, place chips in a microwave-safe dish and cook on medium-low heat for about 1 minute. Stir well. If necessary, continue to heat chips, 20 seconds at a time, until they are melted. Be sure to stir chips each time you heat them.

2 Remove chips from heat and stir in peanuts and chow mein noodles.

3 Drop by teaspoons onto waxed paper and cool.

Makes 30 to 40 grasshoppers

Gooey Apple Treat

YOU WILL NEED:

1 large apple

2 tablespoons lemon juice

1/4 cup caramel ice cream topping

2 tablespoons chopped peanuts

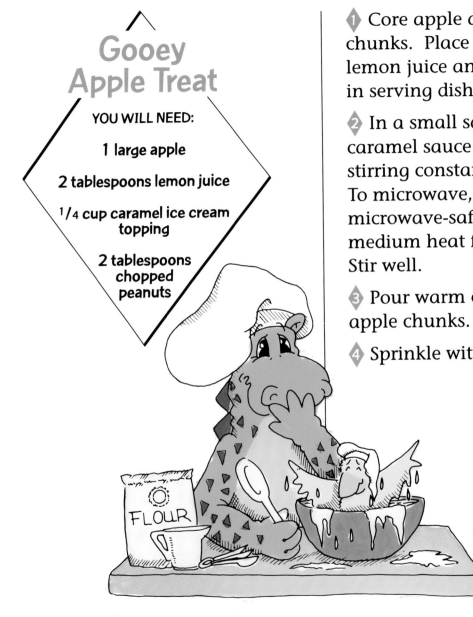

1. Core apple and slice into chunks. Place in large bowl. Add lemon juice and toss. Place apples in serving dish.

2. In a small saucepan, heat caramel sauce over low heat, stirring constantly, until warm. To microwave, pour sauce into a microwave-safe dish and cook on medium heat for about 1 minute. Stir well.

3. Pour warm caramel sauce over apple chunks.

4. Sprinkle with chopped nuts.

Serves 1

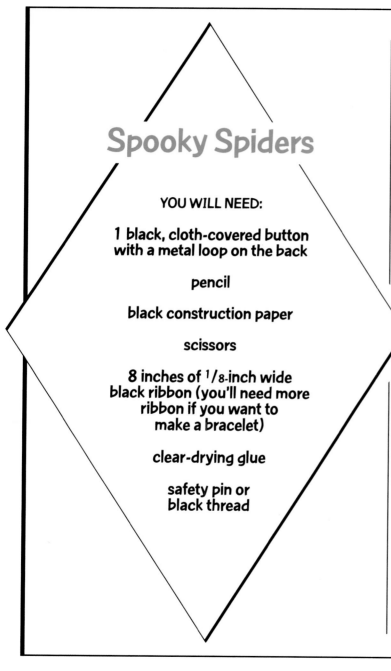

Spooky Spiders

YOU WILL NEED:

1 black, cloth-covered button with a metal loop on the back

pencil

black construction paper

scissors

8 inches of ¹/8-inch wide black ribbon (you'll need more ribbon if you want to make a bracelet)

clear-drying glue

safety pin or black thread

1 Using the button as a pattern, trace a circle onto black construction paper. Cut out circle slightly inside the drawn line.

2 Cut the ribbon into eight 1-inch segments to make the legs.

3 Glue the legs to the construction paper circle as shown and allow to dry before proceeding.

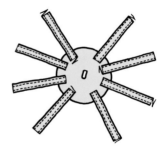

4 Carefully punch a small starter hole with your scissor tip into the center of the construction paper circle.

5 Apply glue to the same side of the circle to which the legs are attached. Glue this circle to the back of the button, allowing the metal loop to poke through. Hold in place until glue sets.

6 Your spider can dangle from a piece of black thread tied to the metal loop. Or you can slip a piece of ribbon or a safety pin through the loop to make a bracelet or a pin.

If you don't have a button that will work for this spider, you can have an adult helper make one for you. Covered button kits can be found in fabric stores.

A Haunted History of Halloween

About 2,000 years ago, people called Celts lived in Scotland, Ireland, and Wales. Their new year didn't begin on January 1, it began on November 1. So October 31 was New Year's Eve. The Celts believed that ghosts and goblins and witches walked the earth on October 31. These spirits terrified the Celts, so the people dressed up in costumes so the spirits wouldn't recognize them.

When the Romans conquered the Celts, the traditions of the two different people were brought together, and some of them were combined. For the Romans, November 1 was an important holy day called All Hallows. Eventually October 31, the day before All Hallows, became known as All Hallows E'en (evening). And that is the day we celebrate as Halloween.

Monster Meal

Transylvania Tuna
▼
Deviled Eyeballs
▼
Green Eye Pie
▼
Freaky Frankenstein

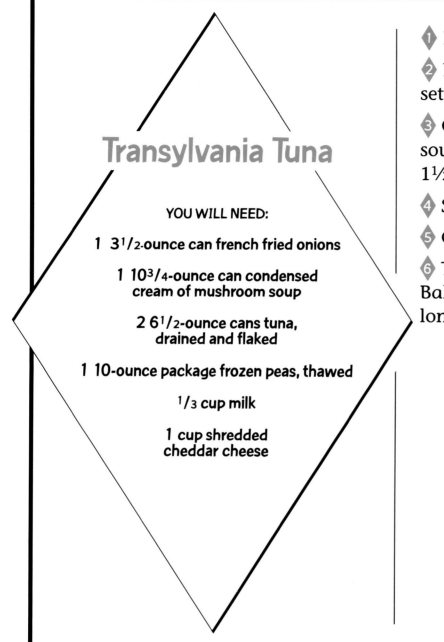

Transylvania Tuna

YOU WILL NEED:

1   3 1/2-ounce can french fried onions

1   10 3/4-ounce can condensed
     cream of mushroom soup

2   6 1/2-ounce cans tuna,
     drained and flaked

1   10-ounce package frozen peas, thawed

1/3 cup milk

1 cup shredded
cheddar cheese

1 Preheat oven to 375°.

2 Measure out 1 cup of onions and set aside.

3 Combine remaining onions, soup, tuna, peas, and milk in a 1½- quart casserole dish.

4 Sprinkle with cheese.

5 Cover and bake for 45 minutes.

6 Top with remaining onions. Bake, uncovered, 3 to 5 minutes longer.

Serves 4 to 6

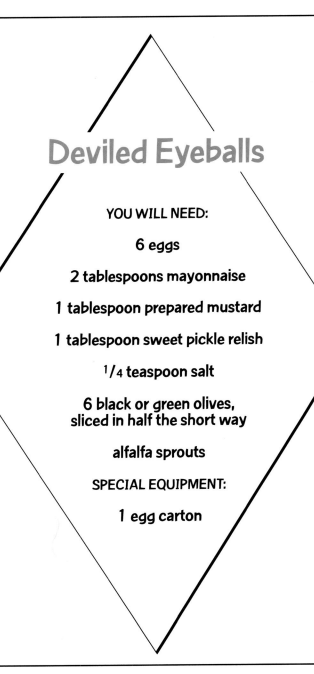

Deviled Eyeballs

YOU WILL NEED:

6 eggs

2 tablespoons mayonnaise

1 tablespoon prepared mustard

1 tablespoon sweet pickle relish

1/4 teaspoon salt

6 black or green olives,
sliced in half the short way

alfalfa sprouts

SPECIAL EQUIPMENT:

1 egg carton

1. Place the eggs in a saucepan and cover with cold water. Bring water to a boil. Remove from heat and cover. Let sit for 25 minutes.

2. Drain off hot water and run cold water over eggs. Let eggs sit in cold water until cool.

3. Remove shell from eggs. Cut eggs in half the short way.

4. Remove yolks from eggs and place in a medium bowl. Mash yolks with a fork.

5. Add mayonnaise, mustard, pickle relish, and salt to yolks and stir well.

6. With a teaspoon, fill each egg-white half with yolk mixture. Top each egg with an olive.

7. Fill each egg compartment with alfalfa sprouts and nestle an egg in each compartment.

Makes 12 eggs

Green Eye Pie

YOU WILL NEED:

2 cups green grapes, washed and dried

$1/2$ cup sour cream

1 prepared graham cracker pie crust

3 tablespoons brown sugar

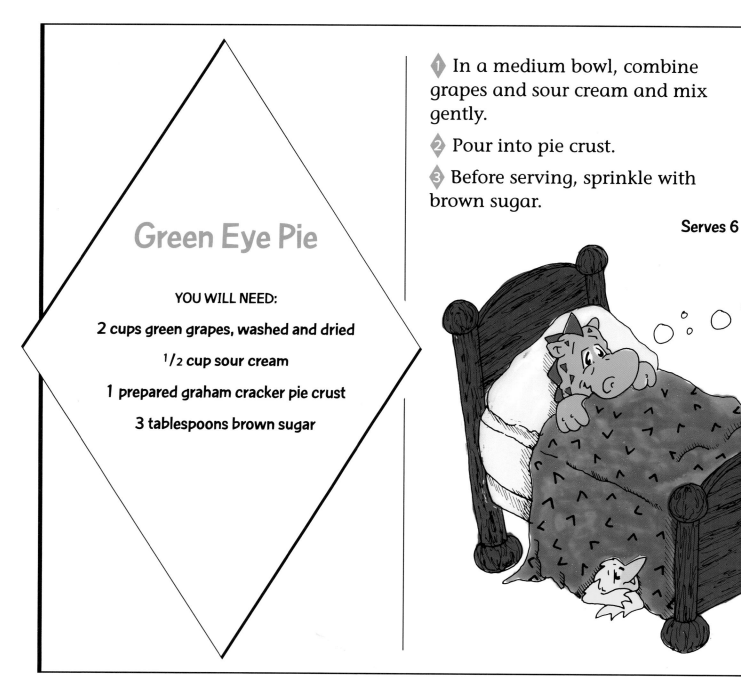

1. In a medium bowl, combine grapes and sour cream and mix gently.

2. Pour into pie crust.

3. Before serving, sprinkle with brown sugar.

Serves 6

Do You Believe in Ghosts?

It is said that long ago a ship called the *Flying Dutchman* was sailing around the southern tip of Africa when a terrible storm came up. The sailors on board were afraid they would be killed. They wanted to turn back, but the captain refused. He laughed at the men and said he was afraid of nothing. Late that night, a glowing figure appeared before the captain. The figure placed a curse on the captain and all of the men on board. They were doomed to sail the seas until the end of time, long after their lives were over. And anyone who saw the *Flying Dutchman* and its ghostly sailors would have bad luck.

Over the years, frightened sailors reported seeing a ship sailing along in the distance, giving off an eerie red glow. The bad luck that followed made the sailors sure they had seen the *Flying Dutchman*. In time, people no longer saw the ship, perhaps because the story is only a story, and not the truth. But you never know—somewhere, alone on storm-tossed seas, there may be a ship full of weary men who will sail on forever.

Freaky Frankenstein

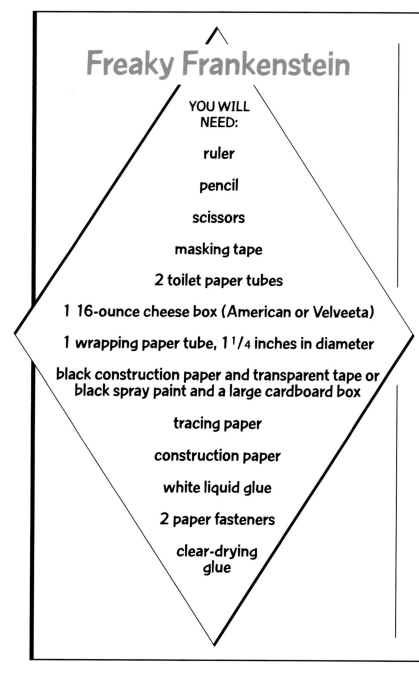

YOU WILL
NEED:

ruler

pencil

scissors

masking tape

2 toilet paper tubes

1 16-ounce cheese box (American or Velveeta)

1 wrapping paper tube, 1 1/4 inches in diameter

black construction paper and transparent tape or
black spray paint and a large cardboard box

tracing paper

construction paper

white liquid glue

2 paper fasteners

clear-drying
glue

THE BODY:

❶ Remove the lid from the cheese box. Turn the box upside down and slide it back into the lid.

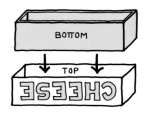

❷ Stand the box on its end. With a ruler, measure 4 inches down at each of the four corners and mark with a dot.

❸ Using the ruler, connect the dots with a line as shown. Cut along this line from one open side to the other. Discard the smaller end of the box.

4 Remove the bottom from the lid of the larger end of the box, which will be 4 inches long. Put the box back together to form a three-dimensional rectangle with one open end.

5 Tape the bottom and the lid of the box together on the inside with masking tape.

THE ARMS:

1 Use a ruler to measure 3 inches down from the top of the wrapping paper tube and draw a line. Measure 3 inches down from the line and draw another line.

2 Cut across the tube at each of these two lines to make the two arms.

THE LEGS:

The legs are made out of the two toilet paper tubes.

THE NECK:

1 Use a ruler to measure 1 inch down from the top of the remaining wrapping paper tube and make a line.

2 Cut across the tube at the line to make the neck.

THE HEAD:

1 Place tracing paper on top of figure D on page 48 and trace. Cut out tracing paper pattern. Place pattern on construction paper and trace around it. Cut out construction paper head.

2 Mark construction paper with dots pictured on pattern. Draw lines to connect dots as shown. Fold on these lines, keeping the lines on the inside of the folds.

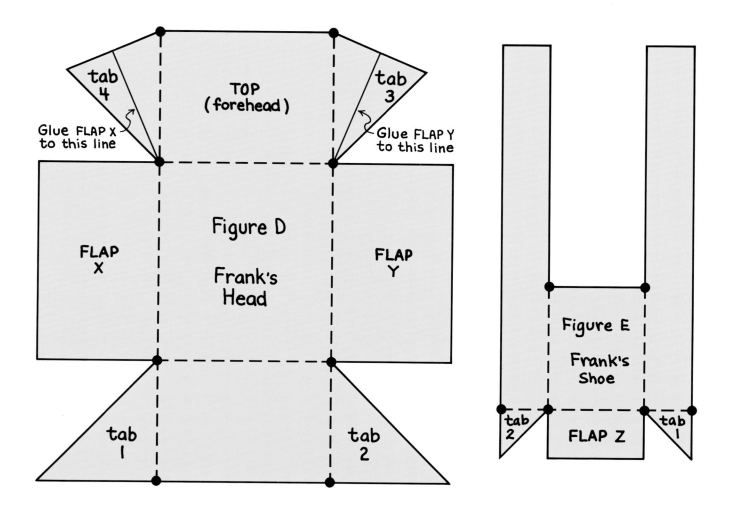

tab 4

TOP (forehead)

tab 3

Glue FLAP X to this line

Glue FLAP Y to this line

FLAP X

Figure D

Frank's Head

FLAP Y

tab 1

tab 2

Figure E

Frank's Shoe

tab 2

FLAP Z

tab 1

3 To form the bottom of the head, glue tab 1 to flap X and tab 2 to flap Y with white liquid glue. The tabs should be glued to the inside. You will end up with a right-angled edge.

4 To form the forehead, glue tab 3 to flap X and tab 4 to flap Y at an angle as shown. The tabs should be glued to the inside.

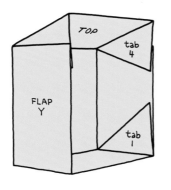

THE SHOES:

1 Place tracing paper on top of figure E on page 48 and trace. Cut out tracing paper pattern. Place pattern on construction paper and trace around it. Move pattern and trace around it a second time. Cut out construction paper shoes.

2 Mark each shoe with dots pictured on pattern. Draw lines to connect dots as shown. Fold on these lines, keeping the lines on the inside of the folds.

3 On each shoe, glue tab 1 and tab 2 to flap Z. The tabs should be glued to the inside with white liquid glue.

There are two ways to give Frank his black suit. You can cover his body, arms, and legs using black construction paper and transparent tape. Or you can have an adult helper spray paint the body parts black. To paint the body parts, first place them in a large cardboard box. Carefully spray the parts with spray paint, being sure to spray all sides. Let body parts dry before continuing.

TO ASSEMBLE:

1 Use a ruler to measure ½ inch down from the top of each of the tube arms and mark with a dot. Using your scissor point, make a small puncture hole on each of these dots.

2 Measure ½ inch down the side of the trunk as shown and mark with a dot. Try to center the dot between the two edges of the body. Repeat on other side.

3 Using your scissor point, make a small puncture hole on each of these dots. Take a paper fastener and insert it into a tube arm from the inside out at the puncture point.

4 Slide the fastener ends into the puncture hole of the trunk. Carefully slide your hand up into the box from the open end and spread the ends to flatten them. Repeat to attach second arm.

5 The legs are attached to the open end of the trunk with masking tape. Apply the tape to one end of each toilet paper tube on both sides as shown. Make sure the ends of the tape extend beyond the end of the tube to form tabs.

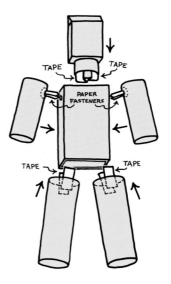

6 Slide the tape tabs into the open trunk, one leg at a time, and use a ruler end to press the tape to the inside trunk surface, front and back.

7 Apply two pieces of tape to the inside of the neck as you did with the legs. Bend the tape so the sticky side faces down as shown and press neck onto top of body.

8 Apply a thin line of clear-drying glue along the edge of the neck. Set the neckline end of the head onto this glued edge and allow the glue to set.

9 Apply white liquid glue to the side strips of the shoes and wrap them around the bottom of the monster's legs.

TO DECORATE:

Use your imagination to decorate Frank. You can use small buttons with construction paper circles in the center for eyes. Use construction paper to make a nose, a mouth, hands, and hair. Then use colored markers to make stitches and cuts on his face.

Orange and Black Feast

Cheddar Chicken Casserole
▼
Carrot and Celery Trees
▼
Chocolate Monkey Shake
▼
Nutty Grahams
▼
Jack-o'-Lantern Candle

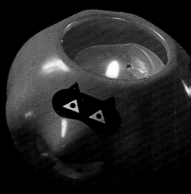

Cheddar Chicken Casserole

YOU WILL NEED:

1 10-ounce can
cream of chicken soup

1 10-ounce can
cream of mushroom soup

$1/2$ cup chicken broth

$1 1/2$ cups long grain rice, uncooked

1 teaspoon onion powder

4 cups cooked chicken chunks

$1/2$ red pepper,
seeded and chopped

1 cup grated
cheddar cheese

1 Preheat oven to 375°.

2 Pour cream of chicken and cream of mushroom soup into a 3-quart casserole dish. Stir in chicken broth little by little until blended.

3 Add rice, onion powder, chicken chunks, and red pepper and stir well.

4 Cover and bake 30 minutes or until bubbly in center.

5 Sprinkle with cheese and bake 5 minutes longer or until cheese melts.

Serves 4 to 6

Carrot and Celery Trees

YOU WILL NEED:

4 carrots, peeled

4 celery sticks

❸ Place carrot and celery sticks in a bowl and cover with ice water.

❹ Refrigerate for about an hour or until vegetables have fanned out into "trees."

Makes 8 trees

❶ Cut bottoms off carrots and trim leaves from celery.

❷ Make several lengthwise cuts at one end of each carrot and celery stick. The cuts should be about half the length of each stick.

Jack of the Lantern

Get out a rutabaga, it's time to carve a jack-o'-lantern. You don't have a rutabaga? Well then, a potato or turnip will do. In Ireland, where Halloween began, the first jack-o'-lanterns weren't made out of pumpkins. They were made out of rutabagas, potatoes, turnips, or even beets!

There is a old Irish legend about a man named Stingy Jack who was too mean to get into heaven and had played too many tricks on the devil to go to hell. When he died, he had to walk the earth, carrying a lantern made out of a turnip with a burning coal inside. Stingy Jack became known as "Jack of the Lantern," or "Jack-o'-lantern." From this legend came the Irish tradition of placing jack-o'-lanterns made of turnips and other vegetables in windows or by doors on Halloween. The jack-o'-lanterns are meant to scare away Stingy Jack and all the other spirits that are said to walk the earth on that night. It wasn't until the tradition was brought to the United States by immigrants that pumpkins were used for jack-o'-lanterns.

Chocolate Monkey Shake

YOU WILL NEED:

1 scoop chocolate ice cream

1 cup milk

1/2 small banana, peeled

Place all ingredients in a blender and blend for 20 to 30 seconds or until smooth.

Makes 1 shake

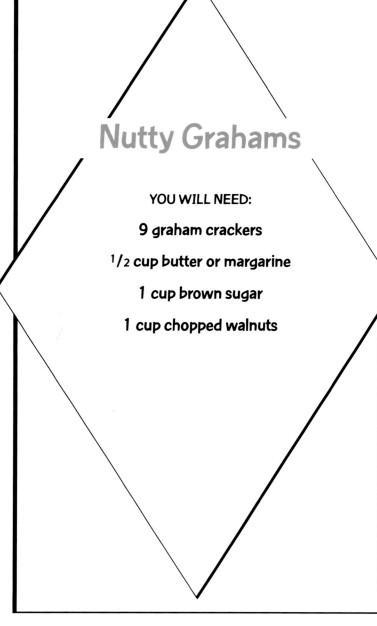

Nutty Grahams

YOU WILL NEED:

9 graham crackers

1/2 cup butter or margarine

1 cup brown sugar

1 cup chopped walnuts

1. Preheat oven to 350°.

2. Grease cookie sheet.

3. Cover bottom of cookie sheet with graham crackers.

4. In a small saucepan, combine butter and brown sugar. Cook over low heat, stirring constantly, until butter is melted. Increase heat to medium and bring mixture to a boil, stirring constantly. Let boil for 2 minutes, continuing to stir.

5. Pour sugar mixture over graham crackers and sprinkle with nuts.

6. Bake 10 minutes.

7. When cookies are cool, break each one in half.

Makes 18 cookies

Nutty grahams can also be broken into irregular pieces so that they resemble peanut brittle.

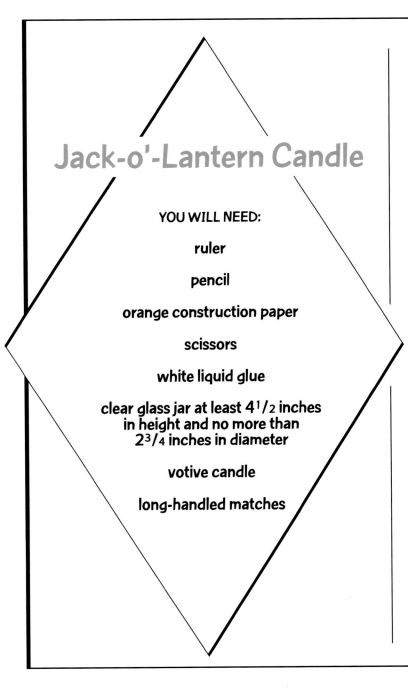

Jack-o'-Lantern Candle

YOU WILL NEED:

ruler

pencil

orange construction paper

scissors

white liquid glue

clear glass jar at least $4^1/2$ inches
in height and no more than
$2^3/4$ inches in diameter

votive candle

long-handled matches

❶ Use a ruler to draw an 11- by 4-inch rectangle on the construction paper. Cut out rectangle.

❷ Fold rectangle in half the long way.

❸ Along the creased edge, cut free-form shapes, leaving about a 1-inch border along the open edges as shown. Open rectangle and set aside.

THE STRIPS:

❶ Use a ruler to draw a 10- by 6-inch rectangle on the construction paper. Cut out rectangle.

② Along the top and bottom edges, measure in ½ inch as shown and mark with dots. Connect these dots with a line as shown. These will be fold lines.

③ Measure 1-inch segments along the top and bottom edges and mark with a pencil. Connect these marks as shown to form 10 6- by 1-inch strips. Cut out strips.

④ Fold each strip along the top and bottom fold lines you drew in step 2 to form the tabs.

TO ASSEMBLE:

① With the base rectangle lying flat, start at one end and glue the 6- by 1-inch strips one by one next to one another as shown. Notice the tabs are glued to the underside of the base. As you glue each strip, allow the glue to set. You will end up with 1 inch of the base without a strip. This is the base tab.

Fold line

Fold line

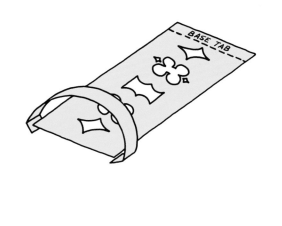

2 Bring the ends of the base together to form a ring. Glue the base tab to the underside of the base. Hold in place until the glue sets.

3 Place a votive candle in the jar. Place the jar in the jack-o'-lantern. Light the candle with a long-handled match.

Recipe List

Beverages
Rocket Orange Punch
Chocolate Monkey Shake

Side Dishes
Cheese Fingers
Witch's Hair Slaw
Lunar Cheese and Apple Casserole
Peachy Spider Salad
Deviled Eyeballs
Carrot and Celery Trees

Main Dishes
Bubbling Cauldron Chili
Unidentified Flying Pancake
Caterpillar Sandwich
Transylvania Tuna
Cheddar Chicken Casserole

Desserts
Magic Center Cupcakes
Frozen Space Orbs
Dead but Delicious Grasshoppers
Gooey Apple Treat
Green Eye Pie
Nutty Grahams

Glossary

alfalfa sprouts—sprouted seeds of the alfalfa plant

beat—stir rapidly

blend—use a blender to mix foods together

boil—heat a liquid until it bubbles rapidly

chili powder—a hot, red spice made from chili peppers

chow mein noodles—crunchy fried noodles often served with chow mein

clear-drying glue—look for Super Tacky glue in craft and fabric stores

core—cut out the central part of a fruit, which often contains the seeds

dice—cut into small squares

drain—pour the liquid off of a food

flake—separate with a fork

garlic clove—one wedge-shaped section of garlic

garnish—decorate with small pieces of food

grease—coat with a thin layer of butter, margarine, or shortening

Italian bread—a long, wide tube-shaped loaf of white bread

knead—mash together with your hands

olive oil—a clear, golden oil made from olives

onion powder—a white onion-flavored spice

paper fastener—a small, T-shaped metal device used to hold pieces of paper or cardboard together

parsley—a green plant used as a garnish or to flavor food

preheat—allow an oven to heat up to a certain temperature

shred—cut into long, ragged pieces

sweet pickle relish—chopped up sweet pickles

three-dimensional—having more than two sides

toss—combine foods by lightly lifting, turning, and dropping them with a fork

trace—copy a pattern onto another piece of paper

tracing paper—paper thin enough to be seen through when placed on top of a pattern

transparent—clear enough to see through

vanilla—a liquid used to give a vanilla flavor to foods

vegetable peeler—a utensil used to scrape the peel from vegetables

votive candle—a short, thick candle

waxed paper—wax-coated paper that is often used in baking because food won't stick to it

Index

A
Aliens, Haunted, 9, 25, 30-31
Apple Treat, Gooey, 33, 37

B
Beverages: Chocolate Monkey
    Shake, 57; Rocket Orange
    Punch, 28
Bubbling Cauldron Chili, 13, 14

C
Candle, Jack-o'-Lantern, 9, 53,
    59-61
Carrot and Celery Trees, 53, 55
Casserole: Cheddar Chicken, 53,
    54; Lunar Cheese and Apple,
    25, 27
Caterpillar Sandwich, 33, 34
Celery Trees, Carrot and, 53, 55
Cheddar Chicken Casserole, 53,
    54
Cheese Fingers, 8, 9, 13, 14, 15
Chicken, 54
Chili, Bubbling Cauldron, 13, 14
Chocolate Monkey Shake, 53, 57
Crafts: Freaky Frankenstein, 46-
    51; Gertrude the Geometric
    Witch, 19-23; Haunted Aliens,
    30-31; Jack-o'-Lantern Candle,
    59-61; Spooky Spiders, 38-39
Cupcakes, Magic Center, 13, 18

D
Dead but Delicious Grasshoppers,
    33, 36
Desserts: Dead but Delicious
    Grasshoppers, 36; Frozen
    Space Orbs, 29; Gooey Apple
    Treat, 37; Green Eye Pie, 44;
Magic Center Cupcakes, 18;
    Nutty Grahams, 58
Deviled Eyeballs, 41, 43
Does Your Cat Sneeze When It
    Rains?, 17
Do You Believe in Ghosts?, 45
Dressing, salad, 16

E
Eggs, deviled, 43

F
Flying Dutchman, the,
Frankenstein, Freaky, 9, 41, 46-51
Freaky Frankenstein, 9, 41, 46-51
Frozen Space Orbs, 25, 29

G
Game, 28-29
Gertrude the Geometric Witch, 9,
    13, 19-23
Ghosts, 45
Gooey Apple Treat, 33, 37
Green Eye Pie, 8, 41, 44

H
Haunted Aliens, 9, 25, 30-31
Haunted History of Halloween,
    A, 39

J
Jack of the Lantern, 56
Jack-o'-Lantern Candle, 9, 53,
    59-61
Jack-o'-Lanterns, 56

L
Lunar Cheese and Apple
    Casserole, 25, 27

M
Magic Center Cupcakes, 13, 18
Main dishes: Bubbling Cauldron
    Chili, 14; Caterpillar Sandwich,
    34; Cheddar Chicken Casserole,
    54; Transylvania Tuna, 42;
Unidentified Flying Pancake,
    26
Menu planning, 8-9

N
Nutty Grahams, 53, 58

P
Pancake, Unidentified Flying, 25,
    26
Peachy Spider Salad, 33, 35
Pie, Green Eye, 8, 41, 44
Punch, Rocket Orange, 8, 25, 28

R
Recipe list, 62
Reverse Trick or Treat, 28-29
Rocket Orange Punch, 8, 25, 28

S
Safety, 10-11
Salad, Peachy Spider, 33, 35
Salads, 16, 35
Sandwich, Caterpillar, 33, 34
Shake, Chocolate Monkey, 53, 57
Side Dishes: Carrot and Celery
    Trees, 55; Cheese Fingers, 15;
    Deviled Eyeballs, 43; Lunar
    Cheese and Apple Casserole,
    27; Peachy Spider Salad, 35;
    Witch's Hair Slaw, 16
Spiders, Spooky, 9, 33, 38-39
Spooky Spiders, 9, 33, 38-39
Superstitions, 17

T
Transylvania Tuna, 8, 41, 42

U
Unidentified Flying Pancake, 25,
    26

W
Witch, Gertrude the Geometric, 9,
    13, 19-23
Witch's Hair Slaw, 13, 16